"I have never wanted to be mystified," Flum writes in one of the startlingly insightful prose works that support the volume's filigree, feathery, flightworthy verse, all hummingbird and hunger and momentum: these poems keep their hummingbird consciousness thoughtful, attentive, in motion, "almost flying," even as its fertilities and their impediments yoke it to our biologically complicated Earth. Can hummingbirds marry? Can they take multiple lovers? Human beings like this powerful poet can, and we do, and we need poems about that taking, and that giving, and those satisfactions, and those needs. Flum offers a starship, an aviary, a sanctuary in half-crowned sonnets and other rooms, durable, breathing, bruised. Ask permission first. Then come in. "Pick up what you need."
—Stephanie Burt, author of *We Are Mermaids*

Éluard says, "There is another world, and it is in this one." Liza Flum's poems ask us to consider what might be proper figures for love the world declines to see. Perhaps birds?—the smallest ones and fastest, darting and head-butting, negotiating or imposing terms. And maybe the right form to express this love is the sonnet—in glorious multiple enactments—or the micro-essay? In these poems, such creatures and forms emerge into their moments, shimmering with life and light. As a new generation discovers not so much how to open and reconfigure love's possibilities as how to imagine and enable the possibilities we have always had, Liza Flum's gorgeous book wings onto the scene and hovers: quick and glimmering, fierce, iridescent.
—Katharine Coles, author of *Ghost Apples*

Hover is smart and it smarts—each poem lands like a dart into the cork of the mind and heart. Pinning ideas with forceps and form, the poet turns and upturns tradition in a kind of zoetrope, faster and faster, animating what was, only moments before, in singular rendering, still. Stillness (a momentary pause) and stillness (the endurance of a thing) makes this shimmering debut a distillation of nectar essential for those of us living in "bodies with wings."
—Benjamin Garcia, author of *Thrown in the Throat*

Hover

Cover art by Eric Nordstrom
and cover design by Laura Joakimson

Cover typeface: Avenir Next
Interior design by Sophia Carr and Laura Joakimson
Interior typeface: Avenir Next and Garamond Premiere Pro

Library of Congress Cataloging-in-Publication Data

Names: Flum, Liza, 1987- author.
Title: Hover / Liza Flum.
Description: Oakland, California : Omnidawn Publishing, 2025. | Summary:
"Liza Flum's Hover focuses on queer polyamorous families, considering
the ways people in radical family structures are both highly visible and
erased. From hummingbirds to stars, historical records, and cemetery
monuments, Flum searches for images to represent lives and loves like
her own and to find lasting traces of queer and chosen family. In the
poetic lexicon of Hover, hummingbirds become emblems of ungraspable
survival and vitality, while records on paper and in stone afford
enduring, though limited, representations. The book explores sexuality,
love, reproductive choice, and infertility in sonnets and expansive
prose meditations. Linked stanzas, which act as little rooms, suggest
the intermingling of bedrooms, doctor's offices, and hospital rooms. The
many forms in this collection claim space, both on the page and in
poetic discourse, to make the intimate outwardly visible"-- Provided by
publisher.
Identifiers: LCCN 2024058446 | ISBN 9781632431646 (trade paperback)
Subjects: LCGFT: Poetry. | Creative nonfiction.
Classification: LCC PS3606.L86 H68 2025 | DDC 811/.6--dc23/eng/20241230
LC record available at https://lccn.loc.gov/2024058446

Published by Omnidawn Publishing, Oakland, California
www.omnidawn.com
10 9 8 7 6 5 4 3 2 1
ISBN: 978-1-63243-164-6

Hover

Liza Flum

Omnidawn Publishing
Oakland, California
2025

Contents

Of such loves unwrit, at the boundary layer
between earth and air,
I feel most clear.
—Jenny Johnson

The moment you cross the line the law has drawn...you no longer belong to the
world. Out there we shall be in the company of swans, storks, and griffons.
—Hélène Cixous

Tableau

On the back porch of the faded ranch house
we watched hummingbirds at the sunny edge of the woods
dive at each other (almost at *us*—their loud
clicking singing made me flinch) then vanish in eucalyptus.
You reached out to both of us
and held my hand and your husband August's hand,
as I paused, briefly quiet. Eucalyptus leaves, in wind,
settle first in one direction, then another. A hummingbird loses
body mass each time it rests. It grows languid
and breathless, nearly dies,
so fast do its small reserves burn in torpor.
What I know to be good
has a half-life, and fades with disuse,
if it isn't always moving, searching out new nectar.

*

On the ass

Today there are small bruises on your ass, not from biting or scratching or pinching like we sometimes do, but from daily needles and one milliliter of hormones.

Now I pull the skin tight over a square inch of your ass and sink the needle in, while repeating the nurse at the fertility clinic: "Wiggle your toes."

Our days have become anchored by this ritual: you prepare a syringe, twist the needle cap off, and pull down your panties in the dining room to show me your ass, then grip the table while I slide the needle into your skin.

Our lives have, in some sense, always been orbiting around your ass. It is tempting to make a planetary comparison but I don't want you to think I am implying anything about the size or shape of your ass.

When we first fell in love, I was so bad at slapping your ass, we both laughed. I settled on other methods of admiration.

I kept telling you how pretty you were in those early days, and then apologizing for objectifying you. I think I never objectified you, though, until I had to find an unbruised inch of your ass in which to administer progesterone.

I have a rule that I cannot write about your ass without also writing about my own ass.

This applies for all nakedness. I do not want to leave your bare ass alone, literally or metaphorically. To write about my own ass, then, is a kind of equalizing.

I admit to having a certain amount of vanity about my ass.

I sometimes exercise in shorts to make you notice my ass. "Indecent," you said once in the kitchen and slipped your hands inside my spandex waistband.

However, I have never truly looked at my ass the way you can look at my ass. It is what I cannot see; it lives behind me. At a poetry reading an audience member asked the poet, "How heavy is your shadow satchel?" The thing I carry that I cannot fully grasp: is that my ass?

The phrase "Cover your ass" speaks to this; account for your vulnerabilities. I wonder if you will hate that I have written about your ass.

The shots hurt. You cannot carry anything in your back pockets for days, or climb the stairs. When I write about your pain, I am writing about your body in a way that feels even more exposed than describing your ass.

I think of my ass as a part of my body that's completely mine. Not like my cunt, which seems somehow shared.

You will take the shots for three months after the embryo transfer. "Stick, baby, stick," we say, crossing our fingers. For whom or what exactly are we injecting your ass? What parts of your body can be, should be shared?

The one time August and I touched your ass at the same time, we were administering a shot and trying to find a location in the upper left or right quadrant where the needle could sink into muscle.

"Side booty, under booty, top booty." My barre instructor has many words for the ass. I never considered that my ass had facets until I found myself, leg extended behind me, using my pointed toes to draw circles in the air.

So exertion brings us against unnamed parts of ourselves and gives them names. Who am I when I hold a needle, pushing it into the muscle of your ass? Benevolent or bad doctor? I do not know how to give this part of me a name.

It's also true that I cannot know you by regarding your ass. You point to the parts of your ass that I should inject today, feeling your own geography from inside your skin.

A tattoo artist once suggested that I get a fiddlehead fern tattooed on the side of my hip, up along my ass. "That's a part of you that's meant to *move*," my friend said, grabbing her ass and jiggling it up and down. I asked for the fern on my firmer leg.

How do I write about my actual, grabbable ass? Is it a lie to think that my ass is only mine?

My ass moves, shifts, sags over time, just like my self does. Which is also not only mine.

If I become a parent, I imagine my sense of self will be groped constantly, like unwelcome hands on my ass. Moms of my acquaintance talk about feeling "touched out," so handled and fondled by children they only want to lie down alone.

When I lie down on my stomach for you, I am choosing to give you my ass to grab and gaze at. So much of what makes objectification hot is choosing it.

You grasping the table before a shot are choosing but not choosing for me to see your ass. The small humiliations of a life that we undertake together, seeing and seen.

If I put my own ass in this writing, it doesn't matter; I choose to expose it. I decide in what light it is seen. In no way is this equalizing.

When I was 19 and sex was just starting, I had a girlfriend whose bedroom floor was littered with books. Once, as I climbed into her bed, I caught a glimpse of *Le Corps Lesbien*: LES FESSES LES COUDES LES JAMBES LES ORTEILS LES PIEDS LES TALONS LES REINS LA NUQUE LA GORGE LA TÊTE LES CHEVILLES LES AINES LA LANGUE L'OCCIPUT L'ÉCHINE LES FLANCS LE NOMBRIL LE PUBIS LE CORPS LESBIEN. According to Google translate, "les fesses" means "buttocks" or "fanny," not ass.

But I thought of "les fesses" as she touched my ass, tentative and gentle at first, and then with hard fingers. "Thank you," she murmured later. I felt like she was touching, not my ass, but the ass from *Le Corps Lesbien*.

To see my ass mapped onto language is to see a projection of my ass, separate from the part of me I sit on.

Does it matter that she was the partner who loved me least? I wonder whether, for her, my ass was a book's illustration.

When I read you these pages, you ask if I can give your progesterone injection to the ass from *Le Corps Lesbien*. So an abstracted ass might become a decoy, a stand in.

"Here?" I say, pressing against your ass with my fingers. "No, here," you say, placing your finger on the place you can bear the injection. I push the needle into your flesh: "It's in. Halfway empty. Almost done." When the syringe is empty I count to five as instructed and withdraw the needle, and you slide your panties back on.

It is a 30-second routine. In this way, I can touch your ass without truly touching your ass; leaving your privacy intact, I have a quick transaction with your skin.

In other words, giving you the shot, I ignore the ass beyond your ass. Even when I grab your ass, there is an ass on you that I do not reach.

I have never wanted to be mystified. "Stand in the mystery," a poet once told me. Love, death, marriage: no real mystery is diminished when regarded straight on. Together every afternoon, in the dining room, we stand gazing straight into this mystery: we are trying for a baby by injecting your ass with hormones.

I am standing close behind you with one hand on the small of your back and the other cradling a syringe. I am looking at your ass straight on.

I admired a teacher. In his poems, women's bodies are portals to the divine. I wrote poems like his, praising women. I learned I was queer this way. It took me years to realize he was looking at my ass the whole time.

When I visited him in the nursing home, he rose from his wheelchair to kiss my hand. I read him books. A nurse bathed him and wiped his ass. He ate tiny bites of lemon bar from my friend's fingers. In the end, his body was no longer his alone. One day he ran through the hallways brandishing his penis as if to say, *Mine!*

And of course, it is easier for me to write of a man's ass than a woman's ass. Which is not a comparison of beauties. When I describe a man's ass, I do not feel the weight of millennia of looks and words behind my eyes, on my tongue.

When I look at your ass, are my eyes ever wholly mine?

You say that my desire to write about the ass is like my love of saying "fuck" and describing bugs in poems. "You love to break a tiny taboo," you say, rendering me seen.

The fabled lost child is identified by the shape and color of a birthmark on his ass. We might be seen in any dimple or mole, any patch of rough skin. Still, I will not describe your ass, or mine.

The injection makes a surface into a depth. It pushes beyond your ass into the unseen. This is biological fact, not mystification.

Did I have an ass before it was imagined, or named?

I would like to get past "the ass." To locate each other through the words we've been given; then to push beyond that surface, into a wordless space. Where my ass is not my ass but a shape and skin.

Bending and extending my leg behind me, I reach out as the barre instructor tells me and place my own hand on my ass. I can feel under my hand how hard I am working.

You drift into the room to watch "the show," as you call it, brushing your fingers across my ass as you walk into the dining room. Of my manifold asses, which one are you touching? Then you lift a syringe to prepare another day's injection.

*

Memorial to a marriage

after Patricia Cronin

It must be their feet tangled past the hem of the blanket
(a big toe pressed to the top of a pale, carved foot)
that make me pause, scroll back to this image:
      two women embracing in marble, hair loose,
      eyes closed: their polished mouths smiling.

I touch the picture and their bed fills the screen: life
crosses their likeness in this public cemetery. Grass brushes
their pallet: a tree casts leaf-dapple across their shoulders,
      and a little pool of rainwater gathers in the furrow
      between their bellies. I want to call you (from the other

side of the house): *look* at this, their bed is our threadbare
blanket with blue flowers and flattened pillows: I can find us
all over their particulars: one's chin and another's chest:
      my stomach, your hip: my shin against your shin:
      but you are reading, alone in your bath, in a cloud

of your own breath, in a nakedness that doesn't include me.
They exist. This marriage exists. What does it mean to carve
living things in stone? *(2002-eternity.)* I have lived small eternities:
      dazzling afternoons on ferries, crossing cold waters,
      at an iron railing watching pine trees pass (*Just as you feel*

when you look on the river and sky, so I felt), I learned to leap
across distance: I wished: I said, "From your mouth to God's ear."
And I have wanted to live behind that ear, too, tucked like a flower
      in a fold of eternity. On my screen a small leaf
      sets sail across the water between their bellies, sallying

along these sleeping lovers' shores. Didn't Whitman say queers

should stand on the shoreline calling, "I was, I am" to journeyers
from the future, as they sail past us in paper boats? I will: I do.
      "What I can't have in life, I will have in death," the artist
      says: a marriage, seen. Is this what living in public means?

And what is our life in public? We drop hands. You and I
and August have no portrait or family name. In a million
iterations of lords and ladies holding hands on their marble
      caskets, what will survive of *us* is almost nothing: still,
      maybe a glimpse: these brides' bodies are glittering,

offset against grass. They establish themselves as the land.
Oak leaves nestle between one's chin and another's chest.
Their marble shoulders are freckled with acid rain. I want
      to shelter here, in their bed's visibility: they let us be seen
      while keeping our privacy: we leap from *now* to *someday*

to escape. I go upstairs and find you in the water. I undress
and climb in. We barely fit together, thigh to shin,
knee to knee. Around us, ripples in concentric circles spread
      to the basin's edge and then return to us
      shimmering: we are what we were setting out to see.

Poem to August

I feel strange writing this,
when I will go downstairs and see you
in the kitchen. Offering me coffee.
Is there really more to this
than an open field where any
two strangers might meet?
Between us tall grass in which
there is something living.
Sparrows, mice. In summer,
fireflies. We share
a place: love for the same person,
each different. But does loving her
give us common places
to walk? Are we two people
who have lived in the same city
at different times? No. A person
is not a city. Do two
people in the same city
find each other every day
tending the same tree? Or two
people see the same meteor,
or two people sitting together
feel a small earthquake, and
meet eyes, fall silent, as the brief
shaking stops: *Yes, I also felt it.*
I lived through it. We were both there.
Like the lunch when our beloved
exclaimed that she didn't understand
what was so great about that city,
the one she had never visited,
and we glanced at each other

over our sandwiches, both smiling
a little, almost laughing: that was her.

Model home

Hummingbirds make nests of spider silk
and lichen, which are tightknit and tough
but can stretch open around bone and fluff
to enclose growing hatchlings. If I had milk,
if I had money, or could pluck
the world of stretchable stuff, I would love
giving some small bodies shelter. I have seen enough
hummingbird nests to guess what it takes:
from a distance the nests seem made of flowers,
but the lichens have no petals or pollen.
They are as rough as scales or dried skin,
and when the birds grow bigger, the spider
silk tangles them in its net—suspended and falling.
Hanging on by a see-through thread is almost flying.

Cradle song for a frozen embryo

At first there was no home
in the world for you, contentious cells.
On a cold slide, first one, then two,
then eight cells made up all of you.
Ice was your pillow.

I did as I was taught to:
I filled a poem with little rooms
and I walked through all of them,
heel to toe. A foot was a human foot.
I thought the rooms were filled with you.
Ice was my pillow.

Now we who summoned you
huddle in a snowfall exhaling
a virus that won't let go.
Our bodies were riven long before you,
and yours will be too.
We have this pill to swallow.

And little swallow, what will become of you?
You have pecked the gold leaf and jewels
from the prince's statue.
What was gleaming is now base metal,
the earth an icy pillow.

We still want to show it to you:
the dried riverbeds.
The city built like a long line in the sand.
The high-speed train that will never run close to you.

And ice was the pillow
for the oysters I ate by the kilo
with a woman who was almost mother to you.
When she and I parted I cried.
For three years, I cried myself blue,

until I was a sapphire butterfly over a meadow.
Then I never imagined you
would be a butterfly too.
You wait suspended in a glass case, but I believe
I can reanimate you.
I'll build a child from snow.

Nuptial dive

A man and a woman jump from a plane

on TV together, strapped to instructors

      like babies on parents' chests: they fall

   face-first through blue atmosphere, cameras

catching their screams, then fields:

     in the landing zone the man tries standing,

tumbles on his back: then they kiss in the grass

    under lenses: these two in their dropped

nest of parachutes, entwined arms: "Love

     comes from falling," say love's manufacturers:

      but the hummingbird's nuptial dive

is obsessive. He flies over the female, again,

     again, grazing her head, then he zooms, climbs

   70 feet, plummets to hover above her crown.

In the book on my lap this flight is hand-drawn:

   X marks the female, treasure and cipher. I study

the flightpath. In the picture it looks like a fishhook,

and he rises as if he were a fish, caught, reeled in.

Does the air burn him, too? What

compels him? The bird flies up, yes,

but is it also love that yanks him? Or need? Is X

glad to see him? Is she afraid?

When I chose you, it felt like a jump

into nothing. It was not to impress you. It was hardly choosing.

Like standing on the high dive. To return to our life

happening below I had to jump. I only remember

how poorly I did it. The rough board under my toes

as I stepped forward. How I fell alone.

How the water lifted around me on impact like a veil.

* *

I never told you my grandmother

was a trick diver. Her act: Disappearing

Mermaids. The secret: to stay submerged

in an airtight chamber, counting to 100, then rise

with a smile, arms spread,

amid ripples. Applause. Over and over.

I found the room underwater—meet me there.

Family names

Our collective nouns are wishes. A charm, a bouquet,
a tune of hummingbirds. We won't admit how they act.
At the feeder, a hummingbird slams another bird's body
with its rainbow head, shrieking. There is no exact
noun for what they add up to. No coercion
of hummingbirds, no clamor. Only glitter. I know
if we are what you make of us, we are a misdirection
of family. It was New Years. Fields covered in snow
made the diner warmer. I passed a forkful of cornbread
to August. Then a gust of greetings—friends from work—
swept toward us. I dropped your hand: "family friend."
Birds that travel together are a cloud, a collection, a flock.
A shimmer of hummingbirds is my favorite collective noun.
They all have a right to the word, together and alone.

A lover who has other lovers

I couldn't start the gas fire
in our hourly hotel room.
I tried to turn it on, knowing
it was just the illusion of kindling,
fuel summoned by a button
and just as suddenly gone,
logs fuzzy with dust.
It's important to cultivate
many sources of dopamine;
pay visits to pleasures
without lingering. I liked
that fireplace: it promised
to light all over
from a dozen openings.
Now I can't stop imagining
your body waxing
in the borrowed light
filling the cool hotel room—
though I try to imagine Sara sleeping,
or mornings spent writing,
or driving through snow, mouth
still abraded from kissing.
You swoop and shapeshift.
But I'm still kneeling
on the gray hotel carpet, pressing
this same damn button.

Chimera

A dress of plumes: anything to own
a shining thing. To wrap yourself in its skin:
half-rubythroat, half-human. The famous gown
sewn from 3,000 skins of Brazilian
hummingbirds must have shimmered in light,
draping heavily over the body it hid,
till the woman was Iris: about to take flight
off the earth she washed in color. A rainbow slid
on the marble floor as she waltzed. Now, a stolen feather,
we whisper, costs years of your life. Forgive
this wanting. I'm watching a hummingbird hover
by a feeder in a tangle of flowers: inquisitive, alive.
I'd give—how much? to own its brilliance
(gorget and head scattering iridescence), or to let it pass.

What vanishes and what remains

A father and son spent a winter together
in this run-down cabin: one table, two bowls.
        Now the door is padlocked, the plexiglass window
bolted down, with *S & J, 1992* scratched
in the battered pane. Outside in the living
        history museum parking lot, a headline
        in the trashcan: *The Salt Lake is Dying.*

+

On this footpath, we keep finding someone
else's boot prints. On the hoodoo we see chiseled,
        Leigh Draper, 1917, "like a dog leaves a mark,"
I scoff. You're beside me. "Do you see these names?
All men." I think quickly of chipping our initials into a cliff face.
        Then you bend and pluck an agate
        whose rough bud hides crystals.

+

If we could just keep our bodies like flowers
pressed inside thick books of earth—but "there
        are fossils everywhere," you say: the desert
holds volumes, and I am a poor librarian.
Like the rancher who said of Bryce, "It's a hell of a place
        to lose a cow." We freeze in dinosaur footprints
        to see lizards among the stones.

+

We drove to the cabin once with August.
We could have been any kind of kin
            in the carpool lane. Eyelids fluttering,
I napped in the backseat while you pointed to birds
off the causeway: gulls, a pelican. I saw just light's
            rippling redactions. You stopped, windows down,
            by the hummingbirds, to watch them hover and dart.

Firecrown

starthroat barbthroat firethroat
rubythroat blossomcrown hermit
woodnymph empress sylph coquette
blue black rainbow amethyst white
-bellied cinnamon-throated mango
sungem sapphire tourmaline glow
fiery topaz emerald jewelfront
trainbearer golden-crown golden-throat
metaltail sicklebill visorbearer
trainbearer helmetcrest sabre
-wing puffleg velvet-browed black-eared
white-whiskered rainbow-bearded
sooty scaly tufted shear-tailed sapphire
mountaingem snowcap hillstar woodstar

*

Portrait of the chosen family with lines from a living will, a hospital visitation authorization, and a health care proxy

When I was eight, I walked through Mountain View Cemetery with my parents, picking and sucking on sour grass. At the hilltop we sat on the steps of crypts. I loved best a pyramid bearing a woman's bronze portrait: "Enie. Dearly beloved wife." She looked west, toward the San Francisco Bay, where red and blue freighters endlessly arrived.

Among those graves I looked for kinship's trace: wife, mother, daughter, son. Even as a child, I was appalled by the graves marked only "Wife." No name, even in death? But likewise—even in death, who appears without a family? In the marriage equality decision, Obergefell v. Hodges, the plaintiffs were "strangers in death," with no name of a beloved on their death certificates: ...*a state-imposed separation Obergefell deems "hurtful for the rest of time."*

You asked me to be part of your family for the rest of time. I said yes as the stones at the center of the Spiral Jetty unfurled around us with galaxy arms, and the lake stretched starrily before us, and our small dog turned in my arms like a moon. I was thirty and giddy. You were married to August, as you'd been for ten years before proposing this to me.

What did I say yes to? I would have chosen to live with only you forever. To be part of a family is bigger, darker, like the sky. Do the stars know they are part of a constellation? Most stars form in clusters, born from stellar nebulae. We call these star families, and they resist the stories we tell about their shapes. Sometimes they orbit one another; they have twins, triplets, and companions. As they age, they separate. This has nothing to do with the stories we tell about stars on Earth. *I, Liza Flum, being of sound mind, willfully and voluntarily make known my desires....*

*

Whatever stories I write, my language makes us separate. An editor flags my use of the word "wife" to describe you, the woman I love. She says this word is "a wish rather than a description," that I invoke an impossible marriage as it slips away. A wedding vow, I've read, is the most powerful act of language. When I first wrote about us I thought I could speak us into wedlock.

Jonathan Culler paraphrases J.L. Austin: "When, in a wedding ceremony, the priest or civil official asks, 'Do you take this woman to be your lawful wedded wife?' and I respond 'I do,' I do not describe anything, I *do* it." But, he continues, "If I say 'I do,' I may not succeed in marrying—if, for example, I am married already...the utterance will 'misfire'...."

I wanted it to be enough to say, *Yes.* But does the state or your husband take the word "wife" from my mouth? And why should words "misfire," not bend, break, dilate, fizzle out? Like stars, can words die?

Many star families don't have names. Because of this, I've learned, you can buy a star easily. Choose a name; inscribe it in the Star Registry; you will receive a Free Photo Book. Star families are recorded by sentimentalists, who believe, as I did once, that love is best expressed on paper. *The Declarant may revoke this orally or in writing or by any act evidencing a specific intent....Examples of such acts are tearing up this paper.*

*

At first, I simply wanted to be in the presence of your marriage, the way anyone wants to be close to a sacred mystery.

I once knelt on the asphalt in front of the sand hill crane exhibit in Salt Lake City's Tracy Aviary for an hour, watching two mated birds dip their long heads into the reeds. They looked like they loved each other, although their wings had been broken for ten years, and they couldn't leave. I gazed like a supplicant: *I grant my Agent full power to make decisions for me to the same extent that I could make such decisions for myself if I had the capacity....*

The word *mustikós* means to be connected with what is private, secret. For the ancient Greeks, a mystery was also a rite; you could be a mystery's participant. I learned to participate in your privacy. For your tenth anniversary I wrote you a card that sits on our mantle: "I am grateful to have this front-row seat." That day I watched as the congratulations poured in from people who didn't know my name.

When did I stop feeling like a witness? When did we shift from two separate commitments to a web? One day we found ourselves both knit together and separate like the tangled roots of floating reeds. Then I couldn't leave.

*

You once spent a week in the hospital. Your mother, August and I pulsed through the hallways like doomed stars. In the hospital bed, I sat behind you, leaning against your bare back in the open gown. I loosened the braid your mother had plaited the night before. Then I finger-combed your hair until it was smooth and braided it again.

In this section, you can state what kind of treatment you want or do not want and under what circumstances you want these decisions to be made.

Patricia Cronin, the sculptor of "Memorial to a Marriage," says that our chosen families are revealed at our lives' ends: advance directives, powers of attorney, wills. When you were hospitalized, I drifted through the corridors on a current of visitor badges and heedless nurses and smiles.

When the doctor asked who I was, he quickly offered, "family friend." On the last day, before we took you home, he asked me, "What is your name?"

*

In the lakeside town, on a weekend trip, I saw two names in the cemetery—Mabel LaFrance and Florence Traphagan—etched into the same stone. 1890-1964. 1894-1970. I called out to you, the way I do, crying "lesbians!" as if sighting a rare bird.

To stargaze, find a vantage: high, outside the city, no lights. Then look for patterns, outlines you slowly recognize.

That night in our dark room, bathed in my phone's light, I brushed through posts until I paused at an old photograph. Under my hand's shadow, a woman rested her face against the back of her child's head. Her expression: calm, relaxed. She and the child looked toward someone beyond the frame. I tapped on the picture to keep reading: this is Leslie Miller and her son. The photo was taken by her partner Lucia. Leslie and Lucia lived with their partner Louise.

I paused and pulled the small screen close to my face. All three women were recorded at the same address in the censuses—a house just miles from where I was born. And Leslie's mother Enie was buried in pyramidal crypt at Mountain View Cemetery. I stopped reading, watching my reflection waver in the phone's screen. As a child, I had sat at the feet of this family, eating the grass covering their graves! In the same cemetery I once paced an overgrown plot reciting Whitman. For Whitman, the grass on graves was a medium of transformation, an alchemy.

Grasping the phone's light, I put my free hand on your shoulder to wake you: "Look!"

If the law does not recognize this document as legally binding and effective, it is my intent that this document be taken as a formal statement of my desire....

*

I courted the law when I was young. I read decisions, holding my breath. My first love and I danced around the kitchen table when the Supreme Court overturned DOMA Section 3. When marriage equality was decided, we ran through the morning streets to buy champagne.

Now, when I read the Obergefell decision, my chosen family

appears as the place where imagination stops. Our life is envisioned only in the dissenting opinion, as a limit of possibility: ...*why would there be any less dignity in the bond between three people who, in exercising their autonomy, seek to make the profound choice to marry?*

I can tell a hopeful story about interstellar travel. A generation starship is an ark where families travel together. Explorers set off to unknown systems that their distant grandchildren someday see. When they arrive, their families will be wholly transformed, looking up at alien suns. I can imagine myself free of the very system of marriage this way.

But I always end up landing back in my life on the ground. "Assimilationist. White picket fence," my friend calls my marriage poems. (Six months later, he'll decamp to Europe and, in need of a visa, marry.)

What would living bravely mean? I want to be a craft that doesn't aim to arrive. You and August, as I write this, are downstairs watching Star Trek; the mission of the *Enterprise* is to travel, seeking adventure without map or guide.

*

In *The Transformation,* Juliana Spahr describes three people in interlocking loves. They look for emblems of themselves. They are transfixed by the image of a bird on television, calling two other birds to mate. I turn to her book as she turned to those birds, searching for my likeness.

"It's nice to see how other families work," says our new friend, holding her glass, gazing at the three of us from across a glowing fire. She is surrounded by her two partners. August and I sit at your side. In the warmth of the small flames, we all regard each other. Even in daylight, we are always under the stars. Connect the dots; they are above us as a net, a picture we can draw any way we choose, a family we can't see. *I hereby direct that treatment for the relief of pain should be provided at all times....*

And what are our times? At the synagogue picnic, the rabbi pushes a young queer my way, who listens to me introduce myself, then August. "I was polyamorous in high school," he says, then walks off and dives into the lake. Where has he arrived? Do we live in the past or the future, in his eyes?

"Forget the state. You are real in the eyes of your community of queers," my friend says. The first time I come home giddy from kissing this friend, you corner me in bed and take off my shirt. I hold still while you kiss the freckles on my shoulders and arms. Someone else has just been kissing these same freckles. I look at the top of your head in wonderment. Why these shoulders and why these arms? I have never felt more looked at or more lucky, like a whole sky of shooting stars.

*

On getting an IUD while Sara does transfers with embryos made of my eggs and August's sperm

Plastic Y unfolding inside me, scarecrow
in a cornfield, cold company.
I chose this forked road.
Sex for me

has been lips, fingers, tongues,
nipples, pulsing plastic.
Her palms upon me as ladder rungs.
At the wintry fertility clinic,

Sara takes her pants off,
while Alex texts me, "Good luck and baby dust."
I watch the catheter's stiff
needle thread her cervix on the ultrasound—between this

and the plastic stem that pushed
past my cervix, the difference is a wish.

+

I wished for this: to push, pull, fuck
Alex, the first man in years, after
an abortion ban passes. Tough luck.
At the clinic, the embryo in Sara shimmers

across the ultrasound screen. Who endows
the embryo with "thou-ness?" The Bible
-grasping assholes in front of the statehouse?
I talk all day to our embryo. I won't sail

off my charted course: this nautilus
drifting toward us on an unfrozen ocean
is the fetus: its laboratory conception bodiless.
Sara and I weep while initialing dotted lines

on the clinic's paperwork, casting nets toward this possible
life. Adrift. Of course, we fail.

+

That's life. Of course, failure occurs.
At my appointment, the kind woman with neat hair
guides my feet into the stirrups
and talks to me about fear

as I feel the metal sound penetrate.
Scientists sound the depth of a lake.
My uterus is small, tipped: the pit
of a mango, no, smaller: a plum. A mistake

to think I could accurately imagine it,
or plumb, empty-handed, my body's surface.
The device, still folded shut,
pushes past the pinhole of my cervix

like any heavy thing pushed off the edge
of boat into water, quickly submerged.

+

A boat sunk in shallow water is visible
from the dock. This disaster
sprouts swaying seaweed, barnacles
at our feet. The embryo transfers

won't work. At our appointment, the doctor
prays that angels may enter our exam room. Three
bodies breathe together,
as the doctor smiles gamely,

mask around his chin, then leans between
Sara's bare knees. There's nothing hopeful
I can say about his showman's grin.
I want to lay a whole shopful

of flowers, red blossoms, at Sara's feet,
near the tide-lapped chair where the doctor sits.

+

Past the tidy chair where the doctor sits,
risen above the fertility clinic's little cot,
a huge painting: black, gesso layered thick.
You can't really tell what you're looking at:

you'd have to touch it. Sara says not
to panic when my IUD strings disappear,
curled above my fingers. I can't pull out
fishing line or hook. I tell Alex, curling near

his chest on a blanket, that I've never
touched my cervix. Sistine, it rises past my reach,
receding into the convex mirror
of my desire. I can only touch

a few things: warm skin and a chime
Alex slips in my mouth: *cervix and perfect rhyme.*

+

Slipped up, perplexed, I mouth
brave words about babies. I make predictions,
counting nine months from next month.
I embellish calendars: pencil marks and corrections.

For what? After we lose the third embryo,
the doctor only says, "Go keto."
My father once stood on a houseboat's prow
in the boundary waters. A faint rainbow

arced the lake. He played the flute
like a loon call, until loons sang back to him.
Now my call to a child falls mute.
I once thought, naked with a man,

I could hear a crying child: I feared
that voice, near and uncalled-for.

+

A thing we call for means conception.
In Alice Fulton's "Maidenhead," her white gown
crams the closet: a wrinkled human brain
immaculately meditating on

its course into inland seas. The mind-in-waiting
drifts, its lobes like sails ablaze.
Each embryo we conceived was made in saline,
photographed bubbling on a slide like lace,

a wave breaking nowhere. At the clinic,
we embark: skiff on rough water,
our shadows cast back toward the dock.
This is what maiden voyages discover:

the scope of the ocean, or else the bars
against which your body batters.

+

The cage our bodies batter
is made of paperwork a notary
stamps and signs: Sara and I swear
we're lovers, as the clinic weighs the legality

of a pregnancy with three parents. Or else the cage
is a paper bearing numbers I stumble to trust in:
our chances: little Os: the embryos in storage
like chilled oysters, still pulsing.

One of them pearled. A shell game's constraint
is the fixed number of your tries.
Though I wish a device inside me, I faint
on the clinic table. When I open my eyes,

I say, "I'm fine,"
then sit up slowly and start counting.

+

On the bathroom floor, I sit up, slowly count
to ten, and try standing. Tender
breasts, cramping, my boat aground.
"Never approach the dock faster

than you'd want to hit the dock." Waves of progesterone
toss me into what feels like a pregnancy. I fumble
with Sara's progesterone injections,
lifting the syringe to the light to check for bubbles.

Then I slide the needle into her ass flesh.
Her uterine lining thickens, mine thins. Our bodies
know we want to chart a course, but which?
They keep pointing: a basket, a branch, a bloody

pad in Sara's underwear. Our bodies don't understand
what we might want from such intrusions.

+

What I want: no intrusions, a *Do Not*
Disturb sign on the hotel door at noon.
Alex cool-skinned and grinning on the duvet.
We share pretzels, some chocolate, and two clementines,

still naked as it snows. He asks me what song
I have in my head, what color. His song, I don't remember.
His color, sea blue. In this little room, *wrong*
life cannot be lived rightly doesn't seem to matter

for a minute. Later, Sara laughs at
my neck bruise. In thought, I tuck that hotel room
among the rooms in our own house: the drafts that
blow past each lintel carry several voices' hum

and the creak of footsteps. Our proximate bodies:
closed doors, separate beds. I leave through the lobby.

+

Closed doors, separate beds: greetings and partings volley
across me. Same skin, different touches. My uterus
once felt sealed from the world outside me,
except for the cervix, which tutors us

in porousness. My hands have punctured
lovers' salty skins with scratches.
I send an old lover the embryo's picture
one night on the group text, as surf reaches

inside the sand, pouring through each opening. *Unscrew the locks
from the doors! Unscrew the doors themselves from their jambs!*
When the doctor cocks
the plastic catheter, what living wish swims

under our skins? Two bodies into one:
a door creaks open again.

+

A door creaks open to the desk where
Alex circles and scribbles on my writing.
Between our cities, a storm gathers,
spangling the lake with lightning.

Rain drums the fields around us.
It drenches eagles' nests and sways telephone lines.
"When you come," Sara said once,
"it's like you've been out in the rain,

a fine mist all over your skin." His notes: *Breathe a little.*
This won't grow with airtight
clenching. Let the boat drift through the drizzle
with a raised anchor. There is almost no weight

to an embryo. But I once felt my eggs gathering
like light rain, or a stanza's half-written lines.

+

In a little room I was half-erased by anesthesia,
draped in paper, naked in the chill.
The doctor and nurse chatted easily
while threading a needle through the wall

of my abdomen. My ovarian follicles
were clumps of bull whip kelp, each one bent
under heavy blossoms. The doctor pulled
forth a froth of eggs. I'd asked to be abundant.

Now on the clinic cot, Sara covers herself with paper
like Venus arriving garlanded
in waves. From the exam room's corner, I watch her
flinch against the ultrasound wand

as the embryo vanishes like sea foam. We choose
silence. As if in a mirror, I watch her mouth close.

+

In the mirror, I watch my mouth close.
Sugary coffee at a diner table
after my appointment. One plastic rose
fills a dirty budvase. The only cradle

for our child is a chilled vial.
In my pocket, Alex asks a question and Sara sends courage.
On the TV above me, rainbow sails
on the water shiver. The boats lunge,

straining. Sara told me once to pick one point
that holds steady when wave-tossed.
But nothing's still here. TV sailboats
heave, then scatter. I choose just where I glance:

in the dark screen of my still device,
a glassed-in image of my face.

+

What difference does a wish make?
We chart a course, a life,
that founders like a boat
full of waterlogged chairs. The doctor sits there,
whispering, "Cervix and perfect rhyme,"
in a voice none of us called for.
With vials and needles, our bodies are battered
slowly. Does it count? And what
do we want, anyway, from these intrusions?
We dream with closed doors, separate beds. I leave
when a door creaks open.
Outside, half-light. A little rain.
I see my mouth close in this mirror: a child
with my face, her glassed-in image.

*

Domestication

on a photograph of a Roman grave

Long jaw tipped
        toward a woman's chipped
anklebone, a dog curls

        her 26 ribs around a bowl
of pink glass. This grave
        is love's evidence:

that what lies at the foot still
        might rise and want a drink,
that the owner might rise too

        and find herself walking,
dog heeled, to the land
        of the dead: the dog

was deathless/ they killed her
        the day her mistress died.
So we hypothesize.

        What we know of love
between species we learn
        from the bones:

some in middens,
        in trash heaps, bear the clear
marks of human digestion.

        My own mother loves
and takes in like this:
        she makes a dog's soft, dark

coat her burying ground
        for human loneliness.
I've learned her tactics.

        I hold my small dog
in my lap when I read *People*
        magazine: "I wanted my life

to be about not just me,"
        an actress says, holding
a baby in her arms,

        her red smile expanding.
I want expansiveness. In my arms
        my dog's little body

breathes and twitches
        in, I think, a running dream,
where he is alone.

Second love

Your unbuttoned sweater, the back
of your head: here in my sleep again. You
were a man, so for a long time you waited
for me alone behind a dark one
-way glass of desire. Now, in this slow
moving spring, blossoms sweep

my small yard like a luminescent minute
hand on a watch face, and I wonder, how do
I count the time since I've seen you? Ten years
pile up like petals. Do you
remember shivering together
under grocery store awnings on rainy

October evenings—then eating fruit
on street corners and stranger's steps?
You walked with me to buy a treasure chest
of loquats for the girl who, even then,
I loved. Of course, nervous grasping kept
sweeping us forward; of course, winter

dunked us in salt.
And now you are married. I am, nearly, too.
And I don't want to change
anything, exactly, but just tell you
how I wish a thing or two
having to do with you. I kept the rubble

from peeled fruit and my sweater
you said smelled like a church
or a grandmother. I was wearing scavenged layers

then. I didn't think I ever could love men.
Now a black and red cardinal hops down
our garage roof to our gutter. I am so old

I have become a dog's mother,
a member of my small-town congregation,
and I read Talmud aloud
to the computer screen. I cling
to whatever holds me in this quiet spring
with the gentlest of tethers.

And at night now I sleep running,
and kick, and dream of you.
We once called our friendly, lived-in love
a house we hid inside.
"Get out of the house," I said. "Just go.
See *anything* new." And didn't you?

And didn't I, too? When I go looking, I find
the house we imagined. It leans
in its overgrown yard: a ruin. And I'm reading
how the sages warned us not to wander
inside ruins. We'd find demons there.
Or at least risk startling young lovers.

Inner life

The meditation app on my phone tells me to live
in the scope of my own skin. So I float on a tide
of my breath on this bus. At night, hummingbirds save
nectar stores in their throats, so they can feed
all night from the inside. What I have is my lungs'
constant appetite. The hummingbird, I know, pollinates
a system built to starve her. At each flower, her tongue
looks for life, more life. As stops lurch by, I'm trying to write.
I thought, once, I'd die early. On my desk I kept a picture
of a poet who died and another poet who died.
In the dead hummingbird's stomach researchers
found only spiders. What she could not digest: hard,
stripped down. Nectar vanished: in her throat, an empty pouch.
The bus doors wing open to the world. I still want so much.

Tonight, taking the dog out to pee in the parking lot,
I look at the moon over the carport

and think: five years from now—
it is dizzying—five years from now,
(as he tugs at the end of his rope,
nosing buried smells) more creatures might
be mothers. Stars over the carport
are bright, alpine: like the summit
where I took my sixth-grade students
on a hike: we saw a bear and her cub
in pine trees, and I said, *don't look,*
just walk: mud on my shorts and in
my pack a bag of tampons, all used,
I thought the bear would notice: I am afraid
to say *my child, the future.* Did it help,
did it save us, that no one looked?

Nature photographer

I can't seem to crop my own shadow out of the frame.
A hummingbird nest can fit atop a single clothespin.
I position it beside teacups, house keys, a wedding ring,
a finger outstretched. The nest splays open. No one home.
And I shove my heavy lens inside its crushed dome
of cobweb and leaf. A shock of violet petal is woven
into the nest's soft walls. As if the bird imagined lichen
as a shining thing—like this playing card, paperclip, or dime.
This toothpick is twice as long as a hummingbird nest.
I imagine toothpicks are designed with particular dimensions,
considering the grip of a human hand and the depth
of a human mouth. Such a simple thing is never left
to chance. The length of the nest is half the distance
from my lips to back teeth: the space of a small, sharp breath.

What vanishes and what remains

This fossilized fern leaves a shadow in sandstone
like the tattoo of a fern on my thigh, the span
      of an open palm—my body is marked by the way
you touched me. Our kiss in public, almost invisible,
most visible, lingers, a smudge of spores. To keep the fern's
      living shadow, the gardener instructs us, "pick a frond,
      place it between two sheets of white paper."

+

What have I left on this paper? And what, grinding this old
want against the world's wheel, did I expect? Casting my life
      into the air, to be seen? My life as brittle
as the tendrils blossoming from the eyes of a ripe potato.
I remove the breakable parts. Still, how it grows from the eyes.
      How the eyes have hands that want to reach out, to touch.
      Scribes once said our eye beams would let us hold the world.

+

And how can we hold the world except through words?
"Mars ain't the kind of place to raise a kid," I sing alone in this
      parking lot, in the Salt Lake's moonscape. Elton John
ferries a friend's words in his song. Writing you in a poem,
do you shape my mouth? Your voice submerged in my throat.
      Words of yours like "gum band." The gum band on my wrist,
      that once held flowers, now grasps a bouquet of blue veins.

I sign a marriage license with the moss

Of course, you have sex in a puddle
on this worn stone: your sperm travels
to an egg flung from a wet velvet mass
of more moss. But you're also asexual by choice:
you make more of yourself by breaking
off new shoots. Though I won't get to choose,
I hope you fuck your way across my name
in the graveyard, as I did once, parked
in an oak's shade by Chapel of the Chimes
as Billie Holiday sang, *love is just like a faucet.*
Now, I barely think of that boy, but the view
of Oakland past the graves was lichen-blue.
Beyond our car, deer bounded in pairs
over the headstones, as if death
were no impediment, just a hurdle to vault.
I was seventeen and most of my life
felt like nothing,
but I wrote with a pen pressed so hard
it scored the coming page with white words
like names on graves, ground down
to unreadable limestone divots.
I know I will have a death certificate
without my beloved named on it.
She and I will be "strangers in death," bound
by our un-inked vows. Moss, will you
be my last marriage? When I have no one
as my spouse, can I have you,
making my name lush, wet, and swollen
on my stone? I want you
to retrace my chiseled name with a heavy fist,
bringing letters to life—stay pressed

on me until you are crisp as pubic hair
against the hand that tries to brush you away,
when you are thin as dried ink, even when
you are gray flakes across my name.

Happiness

My personal theory of hummingbirds is nothing
so single-minded could feel love. Their calculations are precise:
they reckon each blossom they've sucked clean
and map their world's coordinates of plenty, emptiness.
In the rumpled bed, full of books and blankets, we curl,
our small dog wedged beside us. I keep finding
more here. How my palm feels like a ripple
under your fingers, how you startle each nerve ending—
Hummingbirds live in strings: flower to flower,
mate to mate. Do they understand a layering of happiness?
They must live in disruption. How one moment overpowers
another moment, drives it off—as at the feeder, birds chase
each other from food—a bright thing repelling another
bright thing. My happiness opens all at once: their ruffled feathers.

.

Notes from private property

Stansbury Island Petroglyphs

We were afraid the men shooting targets
would mistake us for animals, so we sang
loudly as we walked to show what we were:
two women. On a sandy bank,
by a salt canal, we walked in afternoon sun
for a mile, till we reached a herd a flock
a monument to a person bird of a person
taking flight—what remained where we trespassed
(the best taken, in a museum now, behind glass).
Only us, and these painted forms.
We could not touch them. We thought
we were alone. Then two women arose
holding hands. "Are you the sedan?" Yes,
parked a mile back, on the wet sand. They lingered
a while beside us in the dust: climbing and kneeling
among these stones, these bodies with wings.

Domestication

If you find a hummingbird, never
wrap her in a cotton towel.
When she breaks free, her claws
(tangled in thread) will rip out.
So the lost lover can't come home.
So the bird hovers, maimed,
and can't perch. Better shelter her
in a shoebox lined with silk.

Un-epithalamium

for Sara

This veil one-cell
thick on the algae

exists
just to leave:

it detaches gently
then releases

scattering overgrown organisms:

this is what the epithallium does:
it frees

the region
of attachment

from too much grip
of things: parrot fish, kelp

and other invertebrates:
the epithallium is less

rigid than the cells
it lives beside, and so it is often

the site of breaking, as your hand
lets go another hand

to pick up what you need:
the epithallium

lives in pink coralline:
wherever tide meets sand,

bend close

to the rocks. A scattering
of blushes, blushes, blushes,

a gathering
brightness we can't

scrape off with tool
or fingernail.

Coralline live

on every seabed stone, so common
they are forgotten:

on ship's hulls, angiosperms,
tide pool basins, even

cradling other coralline

until the epithallium softly
shakes each one free.

Still life

Stunned in a man's palm, a hummingbird opens
its wings. And they look unremarkable. Pigeon-gray.
They once were too fast to look at: dragonfly
gossamer. Now this bright body is a specimen.
I thought I *wanted* to see a hummingbird frozen
and splayed: my whole life, I've had a bad memory
for moving things. Like faces. As a child, I'd try
to picture my parents with my eyes closed, to summon
—an eyebrow, a chin. But does loving mean looking well,
or trying? Sometimes I make my hands a picture frame
to stay your living image. You're fast, overflowing
my hands' aperture. I squint to keep you still.
"You can't have someone. You just go with them,"
you said as you packed our bags, already going.

Notes

Le Corps Lesbien, cited in "On the ass," is by Monique Wittig.

"Memorial to a marriage" responds to Patricia Cronin's sculpture of the same name. "What I can't have in life, I will have in death" is a quotation adapted from Jan Garden Castro's "Making the Personal Monumental: A Conversation with Patricia Cronin." This poem cites Walt Whitman's "Crossing Brooklyn Ferry" and Philip Larkin's "An Arundel Tomb."

"Nuptial dive" references the Diving Girls Act in Lottie Mayer's Disappearing Water Ballet.

"What vanishes and what remains" contains a quotation, "It's a hell of a place to lose a cow," that has been attributed to Ebenezer Bryce.

The detail of the 3,000 hummingbird skins is drawn from "Fashion to Die For: How Feather Accessories Promote Animal Suffering" by Rachel Nuwer.

"Portrait of the chosen family with lines from a living will, a hospital visitation authorization, and a health care proxy" contains lines adapted from the legal documents named in the title and from the Obergefell v. Hodges decision. The piece cites a Twitter thread by Mark R. Miller.

"Wrong life cannot be lived rightly" is a quotation from Theodor Adorno.

"Unscrew the locks from the doors! / Unscrew the doors themselves from their jambs!" is from Whitman's "Song of Myself, XXIV."

"Domestication [on a photograph of a Roman grave]" contains information, including a description of the grave, from *Domesticated: Evolution in a Man-Made World* by Richard C. Francis.

"I sign a marriage license with the moss" contains a line from Obergefell v. Hodges.

"Domestication [If you find a hummingbird]" contains details from *Fastest Things on Wings: Rescuing Hummingbirds in Hollywood* by Terry Masear.

"Un-epithalamium" is inspired by Muriel Rukeyser's "The Conjugation of the Paramecium" and relies on information about the epithallium and coralline from Wikipedia.

Paul A. Johnsgard's *The Hummingbirds of North America* has provided much of my general knowledge about hummingbirds.

Acknowledgements

More people than I can name have supported and nurtured this project, either by tending to the poems or tending to me.

To Rusty Morrison, for being a guiding light, and for supporting this book in all ways: huge gratitude. To the memory of Ken Keegan, whose vision, labor, generosity, and belief made space for this work. To Steve Rood, for seeing potential in the earliest draft. To the whole Omnidawn family, for being the voices that formed me as a writer.

Thank you to my teachers, especially John Faggi and Nancy Steele; Jorie Graham and Joanna Klink; Alice Fulton and Lyrae Van Clief-Stefanon. Special thanks to Katharine Coles and Jacqueline Osherow, who saw this project through its many forms. This work wouldn't have happened without your many acts of concrete and spiritual care.

Thank you to the editors at these publications for giving these pieces a home, sometimes in earlier forms:
AGNI: "Un-epithalamium"
Best New Poets 2020: "Nuptial dive"
Grist: "On the ass"
Meridian: "Second love"
Narrative: "Domestication"
Poet Lore: "Notes from private property," "Fire crown," "Family names"
Washington Square Review: "Tonight, taking the dog out to pee in the parking lot, I look at the moon over the carport"
Zócalo Public Square: "Memorial to a marriage"

I have been artistically sustained by residencies and fellowships from places including Saltonstall, the Vermont Studio Center, Tent: Creative Writing, Aspen Summer Words, and the Kimmel Harding Nelson Center. The Barbara Deming Memorial Fund also supported this project in its early stages.

There are many literary and artistic interlocutors in this project. Among them, the work of Patricia Cronin, Muriel Rukeyser, and Walt Whitman provided visible scaffolding for these poems, and the work of Jenny Johnson, Maggie Millner, Maggie Nelson, Kiki Petrosino, and Diane Seuss opened up intellectual and aesthetic space for these poems to inhabit. I am grateful to all these voices, and many others, consciously and unconsciously woven into this work.

Thank you to Justine Cook and Mark Wunderlich for giving crucial suggestions at just the right time.

Thank you to my parents, Paul and Nancy, and my sister, Nora.
To Abby, Steve and Marcia—also my family.
To Teresa, for all the years.
To Rachel, for being my special best friend.
To Emily, Mandy and Ben, for being my most beloved community of snakes.
To Amy, Samyak and Alleliah, for your friendship, edits, and encouragement.
To Ezra for entire years of writing and talking. For being the first eyes on these poems, and a visionary reader. Thank you for holding the space in which this project was built.
To Alex, for carrying this book toward its final form, and for so many good ideas.
To August, for building and becoming family with me, and for doing the heavy lifts.
To Sara, for being the bedrock for all of it and the biggest delight in my life. This book is for and because of you.

photo by Quinlan Corbett.

Liza Flum is a poet and teacher. Her poems have appeared in journals including *AGNI, Narrative, Poet Lore*, and *Washington Square Review*. She is a recipient of a Barbara Deming Memorial Fund grant, and her writing has been supported by fellowships from the Saltonstall Foundation, the Vermont Studio Center, Aspen Summer Words, and the Kimmel Harding Nelson Center. She lives with her family in the Finger Lakes region of New York.

Hover

by Liza Flum

Cover art by Eric Nordstrom

Cover design by Laura Joakimson

Interior design by Sophia Carr and Laura Joakimson

Interior typeface: Garamond Premier Pro

Printed in the United States by Books International,

Dulles, Virginia on Acid Free Archival Quality Recycled Paper

Publication of this book was made possible in part by gifts from

Katherine & John Gravendyk in honor of Hillary Gravendyk,

Francesca Bell, Mary Mackey, and The New Place Fund

Omnidawn Publishing Oakland, California

Staff and Volunteers, Spring 2025

Rusty Morrison & Laura Joakimson, co-publishers

Rob Hendricks, poetry & fiction editor,

& post-pub marketing

Jeffrey Kingman, copy editor

Sharon Zetter, poetry editor & book designer

Anthony Cody, poetry editor

Liza Flum, poetry editor

Rayna Carey, poetry editor

Sophia Carr, production editor

Elizabeth Aeschliman, fiction & poetry editor

Jennifer Metsker, marketing assistant

Avantika Chitturi, marketing assistant

Angela Liu, marketing assistant